# John Henry Cardinal Newman

# John Henry Cardinal Newman

## In My Own Words

Compiled and Edited by
Lewis Berry, CO

Liguori
LIGUORI, MISSOURI

*Imprimi Potest:*
Thomas D. Picton, C.Ss.R.
Provincial, Denver Province
The Redemptorists

*Cum permissu superiorum*

Published by Liguori Publications
Liguori, Missouri
www.liguori.org
To order, call 800-325-9521.

**Library of Congress Cataloging-in-Publication Data**
Newman, John Henry, 1801-1890.
  John Henry Cardinal Newman : in my own words / [edited by] Lewis Berry.
— 1st ed.
     p. cm.
  ISBN 978-0-7648-1910-0
  1. Theology. 2. Catholic Church—Doctrines. I. Berry, Lewis, 1977- II.
Title. III. Title: In my own words.
  BX891.3.N49 2010
  230'.2—dc22

                                                                          2010021083

Sources are listed at the end of the book.

Photo © The Granger Collection

Liguori Publications, a nonprofit corporation, is an apostolate of the
Redemptorists. To learn more about the Redemptorists, visit
Redemptorists.com.

Printed in the United States of America
14 13 12 11 10     5 4 3 2 1
First edition

# CONTENTS

# $\mathcal{I}$NTRODUCTION

John Henry Newman was beatified by Pope Benedict XVI during his visit to the United Kingdom in September 2010. A beatification is, in its proper sense, permission to celebrate the liturgy in a person's honor in a local place. Yet Newman's beatification has a significance that stretches far beyond his own country and has implications for the life of the whole Catholic Church—and perhaps implications not only for Catholics.

Two events in Newman's life stand out as defining what he means for us today. The first is his reception into the Catholic Church. It was a decision with its roots in prayer, deep study of the sources of the Christian tradition, and his own experience of what it means to be human. Newman's journey to Catholicism was not an easy one. He learned what it was to be attracted to atheism and the denial of traditional Christianity. Yet in 1816, when still at school, he had a powerful conversion to what he called "dogmatic Christianity." It was accompanied by his recognition of "two and two only absolute and luminously self-evident beings, myself, and my Creator." Newman had embraced Christianity as a revealed religion and God as creator and judge.

Newman's career at Oxford in the 1830s and 1840s gave him international renown. He preached with a psychological and spiritual insight unrivaled to this day in English-speaking Christianity. His "Oxford Movement" aimed to renew the contemporary Anglican Church in principles drawn not from Protestantism, but from the Fathers of the Church. It was destined to end in failure, as Newman's "Anglo-Catholicism" was rejected by his own bishops. But a stronger movement within Newman himself was to bring him toward the Church of Rome. He came to accept that Roman Catholicism was the authentic descendant of the "Church of the Fathers." He entered the "one true fold of Christ" on October 9, 1845.

The second event is when Newman was made a Cardinal in 1879. This exceptional decision of Pope Leo XIII—Newman was not a diocesan bishop—was a recognition above all of the importance of Newman's theology and mission.

What is at the heart of Newman's message? Here, for sure, we find his doctrine of conscience. For Newman, conscience is our way to God. If we follow it, if we do what is right, then we are prepared to welcome and love the teaching of Christ. If we do not, we end up in a circle of self-righteousness and rejection of the truth. Newman was also an important writer about Christian education. He believed in a broad education that taught people how to think independently—but always faithful to revelation, protected and defended by the Church and its visible head, the Pope.

Benedict XVI himself has been profoundly influenced by John Henry Newman. He read Newman at seminary and has always recognized in him a witness to the unity of the Church and to the power of truth. According to the Pope, Newman's life teaches us that conscience, enlightened by Christ and the teaching of the Church, must come before all other loyalties: "Cardinal Newman['s]...life and work could be described as a single great commentary on the question of conscience...A man of conscience is one who never acquires tolerance, well-being, success, public standing, and approval on the part of prevailing opinion at the expense of truth." Pope Benedict loves Newman so much that he officiated at his beatification—his very first since becoming Pope. Benedict's particular devotion to Newman and his message is something that should make us sit back and think.

Newman lived a holy life. The process that declared him "Venerable" in 1991 confirmed that fact. He was unfailingly generous to the poor; he was a man of prayer and had great devotion to the Mass. He was an outstanding priest who lived a life of purity and self-sacrificing love for others, which places him among the greatest saints. He founded institutions that have made their mark on England—the communities of the Birmingham and London Oratories and the Oratory School—and in Ireland, where he founded the Catholic University in Dublin. Yet his greatest witness then and now lies in his call to "holiness of mind": the capacity, through a life lived in obedience to God and to conscience, to think with Christ and his Church. This holiness Newman both lived and taught.

This devotion to "holiness of mind" lies behind everything you will read in the following pages, which are arranged and selected in order to draw on the central themes of Newman's writings. Newman wasn't a "pessimistic" thinker, but he knew that the reality of sin has to be confronted and recognized if we are to realize why we need a Redeemer and why we need the Catholic Church. He wrote extensively on "faith and reason." He knew the power of human reason and that it could be a true servant of faith. But he also knew how reason is too often abused by those who want to escape their own responsibilities before God and man. In fact, Newman knew—with a rare sharpness of vision—the need for our "conversion in Christ." This is a conversion achieved only through "prayer," which demands serious attention and self-sacrifice. The public worship of the Church and the "sacraments" are key for Newman: the instruments of the New Covenant, they bring God's life to a world separated from him. Finally, Newman's entire theology points toward "heaven" and to God himself, so utterly different from the things of this world, but the goal of every Christian.

Heaven, of course, is where Catholics believe Newman is. The process of beatification implies that God has granted the prayers of a person in heaven by physically healing someone on earth. The story of the healing worked through Newman's intercession has a beauty and a power all its own. Jack Sullivan, a civil magistrate, experienced severe back problems in

2000. He was preparing for ordination as a permanent deacon, and his back problems put that ordination in jeopardy. He had learned about Newman that summer by watching a television presentation in which viewers were told to write to the Oratory in Birmingham, England, if they had experienced any favors through praying to Newman. From then on, Sullivan entrusted himself in a special way to the English Cardinal. Days after a difficult operation on his spine in 2001—one that left him virtually immobile—he prayed in the hospital to Newman on the Feast of the Assumption of our Lady: "Please, Cardinal Newman, help me to walk so that I can return to classes and be ordained." He was overcome by a powerful physical sensation and sense of inner peace. He got up from his bed and walked unaided. He left the hospital that day. Months of recovery had been reduced to seconds.

What does Sullivan say about this miracle? During his visit to England in November 2009, he said: "This miracle was not for me alone, but for everyone. It is to show that God is real, Newman is real: he is alive, there is life after death, there is more to life than what we can see and touch and feel. The greatest reality is the spirit; that's the most meaningful reality. We can experience heaven on earth." Newman, who spoke so often of heaven in his life, has spoken again.

Newman's life is a challenge and an inspiration to many. His hundreds of thousands of letters show him helping and advising his many friends; they chart his travels, his struggles and disappointments, his work among famous figures and events of his day. These things you will find in the many studies of Newman's perennially fascinating life and personality. But in this book you find the voice of Newman speaking to the Church and the world—his concerns, his penetrating insights, his love for the truth—his words travel over two centuries as if they come from one of our contemporaries. Let us allow this great seeker of truth to speak to us, and so be educated afresh in the ways of Christ.

LEWIS BERRY, CO
BIRMINGHAM ORATORY
JUNE 2010

I.

# THE REALITY
## OF SIN
## AND EVIL

*Newman* wasn't a negative person. He was full of confidence in the talents and abilities of the human person and in God's power to work great things in us. But he had a powerful grasp of what evil means, of how we can be led astray, and that a rosy optimism is an insufficient response to the reality of our world. But more than this, Newman insists, only if we understand sin can we understand holiness; only if we know what evil is can we believe truly in the love of God who has redeemed us in Christ. So Newman encourages us to know ourselves, to examination of conscience, so that our repentance may be deeper and our faith more personal, more authentic.

–LB

*To consider*...the disappointments of life, the defeat of good, the success of evil, physical pain, mental anguish, the prevalence and intensity of sin, the pervading idolatries, the corruptions—all this is a vision to dizzy and appall.

What shall be said to this...fact? I can only answer, that either there is no Creator, or this living society is in a true sense discarded from His presence...If there be a God, [and] since there is a God, the human race is implicated in some terrible aboriginal calamity. It is out of joint with the purposes of its Creator...Thus the doctrine of what is theologically called original sin becomes to me almost as certain as that the world exists, and as the existence of God.

*APOLOGIA PRO VITA SUA*

*The Church aims*, not at making a show, but at doing a work. She regards this world, and all that is in it...as dust and ashes, compared with the value of one single soul. She holds...that it were better...for the earth to fail, and for all the many millions who are upon it to die of starvation in extreme agony...than that one soul, I will not say, should be lost, but should commit one single venial sin, should tell one willful untruth.

*APOLOGIA PRO VITA SUA*

*The more* a person tries to obey his conscience,
the more he gets alarmed at himself for obeying it so
imperfectly. His sense of duty will become more keen,
and his perception of transgression more delicate, and
he will understand more and more how many things
he has to be forgiven.

SERMONS PREACHED ON VARIOUS OCCASIONS

*Angels can look* upon sin with simple abhorrence…;
and a like simplicity is the reward of the chaste and
holy.

PAROCHIAL AND PLAIN SERMONS VI

*It is in proportion* as we search our hearts and
understand our own nature, that we understand
what is meant by an Infinite Governor and Judge;
in proportion as we comprehend the nature of
disobedience and our actual sinfulness, that we feel
what is the blessing of the removal of sin.

PAROCHIAL AND PLAIN SERMONS I

*Heaven would be hell* to an irreligious man.
We know how unhappy we are apt to feel…when
alone in the midst of strangers…And this is but a

faint illustration of the loneliness of a man of earthly dispositions and tastes, thrust into the society of saints and angels. How forlorn would he wander through the courts of heaven! He would find no one like himself; he would see in every direction the marks of God's holiness, and these would make him shudder.

PAROCHIAL AND PLAIN SERMONS I

*[The Catholic Church]* does not teach that human nature…is to be shattered and reversed, but to be extricated, purified, and restored; not, that it is a mere mass of hopeless evil, but that it has the promise upon it of great things, even now, in its present state of disorder.

APOLOGIA PRO VITA SUA

*My Lord*…can this be the world which you have created, so full of pain and suffering?…O my God, I know full well why all these evils are. You have not changed Your nature, but man has ruined his own. We have sinned, O Lord, and therefore is this change. All these evils which I see and in which I partake are the fruit of sin.

MEDITATIONS AND DEVOTIONS

*The office* of self-examination lies rather in detecting
what is bad in us than in ascertaining what is good.
No harm can follow from contemplating our sins,
so that we keep Christ before us, and attempt to
overcome them; such a review of self will but lead to
repentance and faith.

*PAROCHIAL AND PLAIN SERMONS II*

*Lord, our sins* are more in number than the hairs
of our head; yet even the hairs of our head are all
numbered by you. You count our sins, and, as You
count, so can You forgive; for that reckoning...comes
to an end; but Your mercies fail not, and Your Son's
merits are infinite.

*MEDITATIONS AND DEVOTIONS*

2.

# ℱAITH
# AND
# REASON

*Newman* had a lot to say about "reason."
On the one hand, he knew that its power to
analyze the world—making everyday decisions,
judging different situations, or in study—was
very great. But on the other hand, he believed
that to rely only on reason in matters of religion
was a real error. Christianity hasn't been devised
by our reason—it's a revelation of God. We
can and should reflect on our religion, but we
can't be judges over it. Faith accepts God's word
even when it's challenged by modern ideas. In
the end, what we discover in science, history,
or anything else won't disprove our faith,
because God has spoken the truth in Christ.
Actually, modern discoveries shed new light
on Christianity, rather than casting doubt on
it. But Newman also knew that it's common to
have some difficulty with an aspect of our faith:
he wants us to trust in God and in the Church.

−LB

*What is meant* by faith? It is to feel in good earnest that we are creatures of God…It is to understand that this world is not enough for our happiness, to look beyond it on towards God, to realize His presence, to wait upon Him, to endeavor to learn and to do His will…. [Faith] is not a mere temporary strong act or impetuous feeling of the mind… but it is a habit, a state of mind, lasting and consistent. To have faith in God is to surrender one's self to God, humbly to put one's interests…into His hands.

PAROCHIAL AND PLAIN SERMONS III

*I know that* even the unaided reason, when correctly exercised, leads to a belief in God, in the immortality of the soul, and in a future retribution; but I am considering the faculty of reason actually and historically; and in this point of view, I do not think I am wrong in saying that its tendency is towards a simple unbelief in matters of religion.

APOLOGIA PRO VITA SUA

*Reason can* but ascertain the profound difficulties of our condition, it cannot remove them; it has no work, it makes no beginning, it does but…follow where Faith guides it.

OXFORD UNIVERSITY SERMONS

*Do not suppose* I have been speaking in disparagement of human reason: it is the way to faith…It precedes faith; and it is the instrument which the Church herself is guided to make use of when she is called upon to put forth those definitions of doctrine, in which…she is infallible; but still reason is one thing and faith is another, and reason can as little be made a substitute for faith, as faith can be made a substitute for reason.

DISCOURSES TO MIXED CONGREGATIONS

*Do we think* to become better by knowing more? Little knowledge is required for religious obedience… We have all of us the means of doing our duty; we have not the *will*.

PAROCHIAL AND PLAIN SERMONS VII

*The enlargement* of the circle of secular knowledge just now is simply a bewilderment…When then a flood of facts…comes pouring in upon us,…all believers in Revelation, be they Catholic or not, are roused to consider their bearing upon themselves, both for the honor of God, and from tenderness for those many souls who, in consequence of the confident tone of the schools of secular knowledge, are in danger of being led away into a bottomless liberalism of thought.

APOLOGIA PRO VITA SUA

*The Rationalist* makes himself his own center, not his Maker; he does not go to God, but he implies that God must come to him.

TRACT 73: ON THE INTRODUCTION OF RATIONALISTIC
PRINCIPLES INTO REVEALED RELIGION

*While, then,* Reason and Revelation are consistent in fact, they often are inconsistent in appearance; and this seeming discordance…may suddenly expose a person to the temptation, and even hurry him on to the commission, of definite acts of unbelief.

IDEA OF A UNIVERSITY

*I would maintain* that the fear of error is simply necessary to the genuine love of truth.

GRAMMAR OF ASSENT

*To those* who live by faith, every thing they see speaks of that future world; the very glories of nature, the sun, moon, and stars, and the richness and the beauty of the earth, are as types and figures witnessing and teaching the invisible things of God.

PAROCHIAL AND PLAIN SERMONS IV

*[Religion]* has ever been synonymous with Revelation. It never has been a deduction from what we know: it has ever been an assertion of what we are to believe. It has never lived in a conclusion; it has ever been a message, or a history, or a vision.

DISCUSSIONS AND ARGUMENTS

*We must believe something;* the difference between religious persons and others is that the latter trust this world, the former the world unseen.

SERMONS BEARING ON THE SUBJECTS OF THE DAY

*Though Faith*…is the simple lifting of the mind to the Unseen God, without conscious reasoning or formal argument, still the mind may be allowably… engaged in reflecting upon its own Faith; investigating the grounds and the Object of it, bringing it out into words, whether to defend, or recommend, or teach it to others.

OXFORD UNIVERSITY SERMONS

*Ten thousand difficulties* do not make one doubt, as I understand the subject.

APOLOGIA, PRO VITA SUA

*Faith* is the gift of God, and not a mere act of our own, which we are free to exert when we will.

DISCOURSES TO MIXED CONGREGATIONS

3.

CONSCIENCE
AND THE
TEACHINGS
OF THE
CHURCH

*We find* a voice that speaks within us, telling us what we must do, and what we must avoid. This is the voice of conscience, the voice of God, who speaks this word of truth in the depths of our hearts. It's a gift that is given to every person, Christian or not. But although it does reveal God's will to us, it's so often unclear and difficult to hear—partly because we are sinners and don't always want to listen. So, for Newman, conscience "raises a desire for what it does not itself fully supply"—that is, a person who tries to be faithful to conscience, looks out for a clearer and more complete revelation of God and his will. Conscience, then, leads us to Christ, and to the teaching of his Church. Far from suggesting that conscience can lead us to reject Church teaching, Newman believes that it drives us forward to accept the Gospel of love.

–LB

*What is* the main guide of the soul, given to the whole race of Adam, outside the true fold of Christ as well as within it? It is the light of conscience…Whether a person…has heard the name of the Savior of the world or not,—whether he be the slave of some superstition, or is in possession of some portions of Scripture, and treats the inspired word as a sort of philosophical book, which he interprets for himself…—in any case, he has within his breast a certain commanding dictate, not a mere sentiment, not a mere opinion, or impression…but a law, an authoritative voice, bidding him do certain things and avoid others.

*Sermons Preached on Various Occasions*

*As we listen* to that Word [of conscience], and use it, not only do we learn more from it, not only do its dictates become clearer, and its lessons broader… but its very tone is louder and more authoritative and constraining. And thus it is, that to those who use what they have, more is given; for, beginning with obedience, they go on to the intimate perception and belief of one God. His voice within them witnesses to Him, and they believe His own witness about Himself.

*Sermons Preached on Various Occasions*

*In spite of* all that this Voice [of conscience] does for them, it does not do enough…They find it most difficult to separate what it really says, taken by itself, from what their own passion or pride, self-love or self-will, mingles with it…So that the gift of conscience raises a desire for what it does not itself fully supply. It inspires in them the idea of authoritative guidance, of a divine law; and the desire of possessing it in its fullness, not in mere fragmentary portions…It creates in them a thirst, an impatience, for the knowledge of that Unseen Lord, and Governor, and Judge, who as yet speaks to them only secretly, who whispers in their hearts, who tells them something, but not nearly so much as they wish.

Sermons Preached on Various Occasions

*I am brought* to speak of the Church's infallibility as a provision, adapted by the mercy of the Creator, to preserve religion in the world, and to restrain that freedom of thought…and to rescue it from its own suicidal excesses.

Apologia Pro Vita Sua

*The world* is a rough antagonist of spiritual truth…
What [the world] says is true perhaps as far as it goes,
but it is not the whole truth, or the most important
truth. These more important truths…—the being
of a God, the certainty of future retribution, the
claims of the moral law, the reality of sin, the hope of
supernatural help,—of these the Church is in matter
of fact the undaunted and the only defender.

IDEA OF A UNIVERSITY

*The Church* is the oracle of religious truth, and
dispenses what the apostles committed to her in every
time and place. We must take her word, then, without
proof, because she is sent to us from God to teach
us how to please Him; and that we do so is the test
whether we be really Catholics or no.

DISCOURSES TO MIXED CONGREGATIONS

*Deference to* the law of Conscience, indeed, is of
the nature of Faith; but it is easily perverted into a
kind of self-confidence, namely, a deference to our own
judgment.

OXFORD UNIVERSITY SERMONS

*Conscience has* rights because it has duties; but in this age, with a large portion of the public, it is the very right and freedom of conscience to dispense with conscience, to ignore a Lawgiver and Judge, to be independent of unseen obligations.

CERTAIN DIFFICULTIES FELT BY ANGLICANS IN CATHOLIC TEACHING CONSIDERED I

*If there be mysteriousness* in [the Catholic Church's] teaching, this does but show that she proceeds from Him, who is Himself Mystery…whom we cannot contemplate at all except as One who is absolutely greater than our reason, and utterly strange to our imagination.

DISCOURSES TO MIXED CONGREGATIONS

*Such is the blessedness* of…those who have never given way to evil, or formed themselves to habits of sin; who in consequence literally do not know its power or its misery, who have thoughts of truth and peace ever before them, and are able to discern at once the right and wrong in conduct, as by some delicate instrument which tells truly because it has never been ill-treated.

PAROCHIAL AND PLAIN SERMONS II

4.

# CONVERSION
# TO CHRIST

*Conversion* for a Christian is a lifelong process. We don't become saints in a day. Yet Newman emphasizes the radical nature of the Christian journey. It means putting God first; it means choosing him when it's most difficult. It means accepting suffering for Christ's sake; it means loving heaven more than this world, and waiting for the coming of Christ. Conversion also means growing in our love of God's truth revealed in Christ. In this sense Newman is a supreme example of a "convert"—he sought the truth with all his heart, and when he found it in the Catholic Church he embraced it at great personal cost. If we wish truly to be converted, we face a challenge—but one in which the Holy Spirit makes us beacons of truth and love.

–LB

*From the time* that I became a Catholic I have…
been in perfect peace and contentment; I never have
had one doubt. I was not conscious to myself, on
my conversion, of any change, intellectual or moral,
wrought in my mind. I was not conscious of firmer
faith in the fundamental truths of Revelation, or of
more self-command; I had not more fervor; but it was
like coming into port after a rough sea.

*APOLOGIA PRO VITA SUA*

*As Christ* is seen in the poor, and in the persecuted,
and in children, so is He seen in the employments
which He puts upon His chosen…that in attending
to his own calling he will be meeting Christ; that if
he neglect it, he will not on that account enjoy His
presence at all the more, but that while performing
it, he will see Christ revealed to his soul amid the
ordinary actions of the day, as by a sort of sacrament.

*PAROCHIAL AND PLAIN SERMONS VIII*

*Divine worship* is simply contemplating our Maker, Redeemer, Sanctifier, and Judge; but discoursing, conversing, making speeches, arguing, reading, and writing about religion, tend to make us forget Him in ourselves.

LECTURES ON JUSTIFICATION

*Christianity* is not a matter of opinion, but an external fact, entering into, carried out in, indivisible from, the history of the world...The Church called Catholic now, is that very same thing in hereditary descent, in organization, in principles, in position, in external relations, which was called the Catholic Church then.

CERTAIN DIFFICULTIES FELT BY ANGLICANS IN CATHOLIC TEACHING CONSIDERED I

*Life passes,* riches fly away, popularity is fickle, the senses decay, the world changes, friends die. One alone is constant; One alone is true to us;...One alone can be all things to us; One alone can supply our needs; One alone can train us up to our full perfection; One alone can give a meaning to our complex and intricate nature.

PAROCHIAL AND PLAIN SERMONS V

*To the end* of the longest life you are still a beginner. What Christ asks of you is not sinlessness, but diligence.

PAROCHIAL AND PLAIN SERMONS V

*All through our life* Christ is calling us. He called us first in Baptism; but afterwards also; whether we obey His voice or not, He graciously calls us still…He calls us on from grace to grace, and from holiness to holiness…Abraham was called from his home, Peter from his nets, Matthew from his office, Elisha from his farm, Nathanael from his retreat; we are all in course of calling, on and on, from one thing to another, having no resting place, but mounting towards our eternal rest.

PAROCHIAL AND PLAIN SERMONS VIII

*Oh that we could*…feel that the one thing which lies before us is to please God!

PAROCHIAL AND PLAIN SERMONS VIII

*Those whom Christ saves* are they who at once attempt to save themselves, yet despair of saving themselves; who aim to do all, and confess they do nothing; who are all love, and all fear; who are the most holy, and yet confess themselves the most sinful; who ever seek to please Him, yet feel they never can; who are full of good works, yet of works of penance.

PAROCHIAL AND PLAIN SERMONS VII

*The truest obedience* is indisputably that which is done from love of God, without narrowly measuring the magnitude or nature of the sacrifice involved in it.

PAROCHIAL AND PLAIN SERMONS II

*Why should we* be anxious for a long life, or wealth, or credit, or comfort, who know that the next world will be every thing which our hearts can wish, and that not in appearance only, but truly and everlastingly?

PAROCHIAL AND PLAIN SERMONS IV

*A smooth* and easy life, an uninterrupted enjoyment of the goods of Providence, full meals, soft raiment, well-furnished homes, the pleasures of sense, the feeling of security, the consciousness of wealth,—these, and the like, if we are not careful, choke up all the avenues of the soul, through which the light and breath of heaven might come.

PAROCHIAL AND PLAIN SERMONS V

*Let us pray God* to…make us holy, really holy. Let us also pray Him to give us the *beauty* of holiness, which consists in tender and eager affection towards our Lord and Savior…so that through God's mercy our souls may have, not strength and health only, but a sort of bloom and comeliness; and that as we grow older in body, we may, year by year, grow more youthful in spirit.

PAROCHIAL AND PLAIN SERMONS VII

*They watch and wait* for their Lord, who are tender and sensitive in their devotion towards Him; who feed on the thought of Him, hang on His words; live in His smile, and thrive and grow under His hand. They are eager for His approval, quick in catching His meaning, jealous of His honor. They see Him in all things, expect Him in all events, and amid all the cares, the interests, and the pursuits of this life, still would feel an awful joy, not a disappointment, did they hear that He was on the point of coming.

PAROCHIAL AND PLAIN SERMONS

*Gloom* is no Christian temper; … repentance is not real, which has not love in it; … self-chastisement is not acceptable, which is not sweetened by faith and cheerfulness. We must live in sunshine, even when we sorrow; we must live in God's presence, we must not shut ourselves up in our own hearts, even when we are reckoning up our past sins.

PAROCHIAL AND PLAIN SERMONS V

*The true Christian* is ever dying while he lives;…He has no work but that of…preparing for the judgment. He has no aim but that of being found worthy to…

stand before the Son of man. And therefore day by day he unlearns the love of this world, and the desire of its praise; he can bear to belong to the nameless family of God, and to seem to the world strange in it and out of place, for so he is.

*PAROCHIAL AND PLAIN SERMONS IV*

*A religious person,* in proportion as obedience becomes more and more easy to him, *will* doubtless do his duty unconsciously. It will be *natural* to obey, and therefore he will *do* it *naturally*, that is, without effort or deliberation…When we have mastered our hearts in any matter…we no more think of the duty while we obey, than we think how to walk when we walk.

*PAROCHIAL AND PLAIN SERMONS I*

*Let us* set it down then, as a first principle in religion, that all of us must come to Christ, in some sense or other, through things naturally unpleasant to us; it may be even through bodily suffering, such as the Apostles endured, or it may be nothing more than the subduing of our natural infirmities and the sacrifice of our natural wishes.

*PAROCHIAL AND PLAIN SERMONS VII*

5.

PRAYER

*Prayer* links this world with heaven. We should take every opportunity to remember that we are in God's presence and to meditate on the life, death, and resurrection of Christ. Like any good habit, prayer takes practice but reveals its fruit in a greater love of God and of the Catholic faith. It is a powerful support to us in difficult times. If we don't spend time in prayer, our religion becomes too theoretical or too sentimental. It keeps us close to Christ, and so close to ultimate truth and goodness. Prayer also means speaking to him, asking him for everything that we need. Jesus is our friend, who wants to help us, but he wants us to ask for that help. Let us make Newman's prayer our own: "Yes, my Lord, You desire that I should ask You; You are ever listening for my voice."

–LB

*To be religious* is to have the habit of prayer, or to pray always. This is what Scripture means by doing all things to God's glory; that is, so placing God's presence and will before us, and so consistently acting with a reference to Him, that all we do becomes one body and course of obedience, witnessing without ceasing to Him who made us.

*PAROCHIAL AND PLAIN SERMONS VII*

*Prayer indeed* is the very essence of all religion; but in the heathen [pagan] religions it was either public or personal; it was a state ordinance, or a selfish expedient for the attainment of certain tangible, temporal goods. Very different from this was its exercise among Christians, who were thereby knit together in one body, different, as they were, in races, ranks, and habits, distant from each other in country, and helpless amid hostile populations. Yet it proved sufficient for its purpose. Christians could not correspond; they could not combine; but they could pray one for another.

*CERTAIN DIFFICULTIES FELT BY ANGLICANS IN
CATHOLIC TEACHING CONSIDERED I*

*What is meditating* on Christ? It is simply this, thinking habitually and constantly of Him and of His deeds and sufferings. It is to have Him before our minds as One whom we may contemplate, worship, and address when we rise up, when we lie down, when we eat and drink, when we are at home and abroad, when we are working, or walking, or at rest, when we are alone, and again when we are in company; this is meditating.

PAROCHIAL AND PLAIN SERMONS VI

*Those who cannot pray* for Christ's coming ought not in consistency to pray at all.

PAROCHIAL AND PLAIN SERMONS V

*[Jesus]* is our best friend...the only real Lover of our souls—He takes all means to make us love Him in return, and He refuses us nothing if we do.

MEDITATIONS AND DEVOTIONS

*The martyrs*, the confessors of the Church, bishops, evangelists, doctors, preachers, monks, hermits, ascetical teachers,—have they not, one and all, as their histories show, lived on the very name of Jesus, as food, as medicine, as fragrance, as light, as life?

SERMONS PREACHED ON VARIOUS OCCASIONS

*It is the widow* and the fatherless, the infirm, the helpless, the devoted, bound together in prayer, who are the strength of the Church.

PAROCHIAL AND PLAIN SERMONS III

*As speech* is the organ of human society, and the means of human civilization, so is prayer the instrument of divine fellowship and divine training.

PAROCHIAL AND PLAIN SERMONS IV

*O Lord*...You are ever waiting to do me benefits, to pour upon me blessings. You are ever waiting for me to ask You to be merciful to me. Yes, my Lord, You desire that I should ask You; You are ever listening for my voice.

MEDITATIONS AND DEVOTIONS

*As philosophers* of this world bury themselves in museums and laboratories, descend into mines, or wander among woods or on the seashore, so the inquirer into heavenly truths dwells in the cell and the oratory, pouring forth his heart in prayer, collecting his thoughts in meditation, dwelling on the idea of Jesus, or of Mary, or of grace, or of eternity, and pondering the words of holy men who have gone before him, till before his mental sight arises the hidden wisdom of the perfect...and which He "reveals unto them by His Spirit" (1 Cor 2:10).

DISCOURSES TO MIXED CONGREGATIONS

*When we kneel down* in prayer in private, let us think to ourselves, Thus shall I one day kneel down before [Jesus Christ's] very footstool...and He will be seated over against me...I come, with the thought of that awful hour before me, I come to confess my sin to Him now, that He may pardon it then, and I say, "O Lord, Holy God, Holy and Strong, Holy and Immortal, in the hour of death and in the day of judgment, deliver us, O Lord!"

PAROCHIAL AND PLAIN SERMONS V

*They who are* the pure in heart, like Joseph; or the meek among men, like Moses; or faithful found among the faithless, as Daniel; these see God all through life in the face of His Eternal Son; and, while the world mocks them, or tries to reason them out of their own real knowledge, they are...blessed and hidden, "with Christ in God," beyond the tumult and idols of the world, and interceding for it.

PAROCHIAL AND PLAIN SERMONS VII

*Those who give up* regularity in prayer have lost a principal means of reminding themselves that spiritual life is obedience to a Lawgiver, not a mere feeling or a taste.

PAROCHIAL AND PLAIN SERMONS I

6.

## THE
## CHRISTIAN
## LIFE

*What does* Christianity mean for our daily lives? How does it impact our work, our relationships, our hopes and fears? First, it means doing our duty to our families, to the Church, in our place of work. It doesn't necessarily mean anything extraordinary, but it does mean living every moment of our lives with Christ, having always in mind his will for us, and bringing this to every decision and every person that we meet. We need to bear with the faults of others, be kind when others are difficult, so that Christ can make us into messengers of peace. And we are called to speak out to defend the Church, not being afraid of calling evil by its name. Finally, Christ wants us to be pure as he was pure, turning aside from the many temptations which the world throws before us.

– L B

*If we wish* to be perfect, we have nothing more to do than to perform the ordinary duties of the day well. A short road to perfection—short, not because easy, but because pertinent and intelligible. There are no short ways to perfection, but there are sure ones.

If you ask me what you are to do in order to be perfect, I say, first—Do not lie in bed beyond the due time of rising; give your first thoughts to God; make a good visit to the Blessed Sacrament; say the Angelus devoutly; eat and drink to God's glory; say the Rosary well; be recollected; keep out bad thoughts; make your evening meditation well; examine yourself daily; go to bed in good time, and you are already perfect.

MEDITATIONS AND DEVOTIONS


*Blessed are they* who give the flower of their days, and their strength of soul and body to Him; blessed are they who in their youth turn to Him who gave His life for them, and would happily give it to them and implant it in them, that they may live for ever. Blessed are they who resolve—come good, come evil, come sunshine, come tempest, come honor, come dishonor—that He shall be their Lord and Master, their King and God!

PAROCHIAL AND PLAIN SERMONS VIII

*A person* who is religious, is religious morning, noon, and night; his religion is a certain character, a mold in which his thoughts, words, and actions are cast, all forming parts of one and the same whole. He sees God in all things; every course of action he directs towards those spiritual objects which God has revealed to him; every occurrence of the day, every event, every person met with, all news which he hears, he measures by the standard of God's will.

PAROCHIAL AND PLAIN SERMONS VII

*We are not* our own, any more than what we possess is our own. We did not make ourselves; we cannot be supreme over ourselves. We cannot be our own masters. We are God's property by creation, by redemption, by regeneration.

PAROCHIAL AND PLAIN SERMONS V

*Real love must depend* on practice, and therefore, must begin by exercising itself on our friends around us…By trying to love our relations and friends, by submitting to their wishes, though contrary to our own, by bearing with their infirmities, by overcoming their occasional waywardness by kindness, by dwelling on their excellences,…thus it is that we form in our hearts that root of charity, which, though small at first, may, like the mustard seed, at last even overshadow the earth.

PAROCHIAL AND PLAIN SERMONS II

*Your life* displays Christ without your intending it. You cannot help it. Your *words and deeds* will show on the long run, where your treasure is, and your heart.

PAROCHIAL AND PLAIN SERMONS I

*The Christian* throws himself fearlessly upon the future, because he believes in Him which is, and which was, and which is to come.

PAROCHIAL AND PLAIN SERMONS VI

*While that we* are still on earth, and our duties [are] in this world, let us never forget that, while our love must be silent, our faith must be vigorous and lively. Let us never forget that in proportion as our love is "rooted and grounded" in the next world, our faith must branch forth like a fruitful tree into this [world]. The calmer our hearts, the more active be our lives; the more tranquil we are, the more busy; the more resigned, the more zealous; the more unruffled, the more fervent.

PAROCHIAL AND PLAIN SERMONS IV

*They alone* are able truly to enjoy this world, who begin with the world unseen. They alone enjoy it, who have first abstained from it. They alone can truly feast, who have first fasted;…they alone inherit it, who take it as a shadow of the world to come, and who for that world to come relinquish it.

PAROCHIAL AND PLAIN SERMONS VI

*The Christian* should in all things be sorrowful yet always rejoicing, and dying yet living, and having nothing, yet possessing all things. Such seeming contradictions arise from the want of depth in our minds to master the whole truth. We have not eyes keen enough to follow out the lines of God's providence...which [will] meet at length, though at first sight they seem parallel.

PAROCHIAL AND PLAIN SERMONS V

*Our earthly life*...promises immortality, yet it is mortal; it contains life in death and eternity in time; and it attracts us by beginnings which faith alone brings to an end.

PAROCHIAL AND PLAIN SERMONS IV

*Nothing but charity* can enable you to live well or to die well.

DISCOURSES TO MIXED CONGREGATIONS

*We daily influence* each other for good or evil; let us not be the occasion of misleading others by our silence, when we ought to speak.

PAROCHIAL AND PLAIN SERMONS II

*Love clearly does not* consist merely in great sacrifices. We can take no comfort...merely on the ground of great deeds or great sufferings. The greatest sacrifices without love would be worth nothing, and that they are great does not necessarily prove they are done with love.

PAROCHIAL AND PLAIN SERMONS V


*Prayer and fasting* have been called the wings of the soul, and they who neither fast nor pray cannot follow Christ.

PAROCHIAL AND PLAIN SERMONS VI


*The doctrine* of the Cross does but teach...the very same lesson which this world teaches to those who live long in it, who have much experience in it, who know it. The world is sweet to the lips, but bitter to the taste.

PAROCHIAL AND PLAIN SERMONS VI


*What we want* is to understand that we are in the place in which the early Christians were...—to feel that we are in a sinful world, a world lying in wickedness; to discern our position in it, that we are witnesses in it, that reproach and suffering are our portion,—so that we must not "think it strange" if they come upon us, but a kind of gracious exception if they do not.

DISCUSSIONS AND ARGUMENTS

*The impure* cannot love God; and those who are without love of God cannot really be pure. Purity prepares the soul for love, and love confirms the soul in purity.

DISCOURSES TO MIXED CONGREGATIONS

*Never think yourself safe* because you do your duty in ninety-nine points; it is the hundredth which is to be the ground of your self-denial.

PAROCHIAL AND PLAIN SERMONS I

*Good is never done* except at the expense of those who do it: truth is never enforced except at the sacrifice of its propounders.

LECTURES ON THE PRESENT POSITION OF CATHOLICS IN ENGLAND

## 7.

# THE CHURCH
# IN A CHANGING
# WORLD

*Newman* reflected deeply on the nature and mission of the Christian Church. He came to believe it was "visible"—it has a structure of government in communion with the Bishop of Rome, the Pope; it shows a public face to the world. But he also understood the Church as "invisible"—the Church in heaven, those in purgatory, and the secret bonds of grace that link one Christian to another. He knew that Christians had always been persecuted. But he also thought that modern society had special difficulties in accepting Christianity: people think they can do without religion or that civilization has replaced religion. Or they think that religion is fine if people want it, but that all religions are much the same. In the face of all this, Newman believed that the Catholic Church is the only true bearer of peace and salvation to our troubled world.

–LB

*The Church* is a collection of souls, brought together in one by God's secret grace, though that grace comes to them through visible instruments, and unites them to a visible hierarchy. What is seen is not the whole of the Church, but the visible part of it. When we say that Christ loves His Church, we mean that He loves nothing of earthly nature, but...the varied fruits of His grace in innumerable hearts.

SERMONS PREACHED ON VARIOUS OCCASIONS

*Outside the Catholic Church* things are tending,—with far greater rapidity...—to atheism in one shape or other. What a scene, what a prospect, does the whole of Europe present at this day!

APOLOGIA PRO VITA SUA

*The Church*...includes specimens of every class among her children. She is the solace of the forlorn, the chastener of the prosperous, and the guide of the wayward. She keeps a mother's eye for the innocent, bears with a heavy hand upon the wanton, and has a voice of majesty for the proud. She opens the mind of the ignorant, and she prostrates the intellect of even the most gifted. These are not words; she has done it, she does it still, she undertakes to do it.

*DISCOURSES TO MIXED CONGREGATIONS*

*It is the peculiarity* of the warfare between the Church and the world that the world seems ever gaining on the Church, yet the Church is really ever gaining on the world. Its enemies are ever triumphing over it...and its members ever despairing; yet it abides. It abides and sees the ruin of its oppressors and enemies.

*SERMONS BEARING ON THE SUBJECTS OF THE DAY*

*A large community,* such as the Church, necessarily moves slowly, and this will particularly be the case when it is subject to distinct temporal rulers, exposed to various political interests, and embarrassed by such impediments to communication (physical or moral, mountains and seas, languages and laws) as separation into nations involves. Added to this, the Church is composed of a vast number of ranks and offices, so that there is scarcely any of her acts that belongs to one individual will, or is elaborated by one intellect, or that is not rather the just result of many co-operating agents.

DISCUSSIONS AND ARGUMENTS I


*What is the* world's religion now? It has taken the brighter side of the Gospel,—its tidings of comfort, its precepts of love; all darker, deeper views of man's condition and prospects being comparatively forgotten. This is the religion *natural* to a civilized age, and well has Satan dressed and completed it into an idol of the Truth.

PAROCHIAL AND PLAIN SERMONS I

*Liberalism in religion* is the doctrine that there is no positive truth in religion, but that one creed is as good as another, and this is the teaching which is gaining substance and force daily. ...It teaches that all are to be tolerated, for all are matters of opinion. Revealed religion is not a truth, but a sentiment and a taste; not an objective fact, not miraculous; and it is the right of each individual to make it say just what strikes his fancy. Devotion is not necessarily founded on faith. Men may go to Protestant Churches and to Catholic, may get good from both and belong to neither.

ADDRESSES TO CARDINAL NEWMAN WITH HIS REPLIES

*In the world*...men first glut themselves, and then loathe their excesses; they take their fill of good, and then suffer; they are rich that they may be poor; they laugh that they may weep.... But in the Church of God it is reversed; the poor *shall* be rich, the lowly shall be exalted, those that sow in tears shall reap in joy, those that mourn shall be comforted, those that suffer with Christ shall reign with Him.

PAROCHIAL AND PLAIN SERMONS IV

*In this day* Christ comes not in pride of intellect, or reputation for philosophy. These are the glittering robes in which Satan is now arraying. Many spirits are abroad, more are issuing from the pit; the credentials which they display are the precious gifts of mind, beauty, richness, depth, originality. Christian, look hard at them…and ask them for the print of the nails.

HISTORICAL SKETCHES II

*The holier* a man is, the less he is understood…All who have any spark of living faith will understand him in a measure, and the holier he is, they will, for the most part, be attracted the more; but those who serve the world will be blind to him, or scorn and dislike him…. This, I say, happened to our Lord.

PAROCHIAL AND PLAIN SERMONS IV

*In this day* especially it is very easy for men to be benevolent, liberal, and dispassionate. It costs nothing to be dispassionate when you feel nothing, to be cheerful when you have nothing to fear, to be liberal when what you give is not your own, and to be benevolent when you have no principles and no opinions. Men nowadays are moderate and equitable, not because the Lord is at hand, but because they do not feel that He is coming.

PAROCHIAL AND PLAIN SERMONS V

*Men cannot believe* their own time is an especially wicked time; for, with Scripture unstudied and hearts untrained in holiness, they have no standard to compare it with. They take warning from no troubles or perplexities, which rather carry them away to search out the earthly causes of them, and the possible remedies. They consider them as conditions of this world, necessary results of this or that state of society.

PAROCHIAL AND PLAIN SERMONS II

*If it is* a great work to preserve Christianity in the world, this I think the Church has done and is doing.

FROM A LETTER TO JOHN RICKARDS MOZLEY,<br>APRIL 21 1875

*Where [and] what* is this thing in this age, which in the first age was the Catholic Church? The Church called Catholic now, is that very same thing in hereditary descent, in organization, in principles, in position, in external relations, which was called the Catholic Church then.

CERTAIN DIFFICULTIES FELT BY ANGLICANS IN CATHOLIC TEACHING CONSIDERED I

*In questions of right* and wrong, there is nothing really strong in the whole world, nothing decisive and operative, but the voice of him to whom have been committed the keys of the kingdom and the oversight of Christ's flock. The voice of Peter is now, as it ever has been, a real authority, infallible when it teaches, ever taking the lead wisely and distinctly in its own province…. Before it speaks, the most saintly may mistake; and after it has spoken, the most gifted must obey.

CATHEDRA SEMPITERNA

*Dear brethren*, what joy and what thankfulness should be ours that God has brought us into the Church of His Son! What gift is equal to it in the whole world.

DISCOURSE TO MIXED CONGREGATIONS

*Our Lord Jesus Christ*, after dying for our sins on the Cross, and ascending on high, left not the world as He found it, but left a blessing behind Him. He left…a secret home, for faith and love to enjoy…. Do you ask what it is? It [is] "the foundation of the Apostles and Prophets, Jesus Christ Himself being the chief cornerstone;" "the Building fitly framed" and "growing unto an Holy Temple in the Lord;" "a Habitation of God through the Spirit." This is the Church of God, which is our true home of God's providing, His own heavenly court…into which He introduces us by a new birth [of Baptism].

PAROCHIAL AND PLAIN SERMONS IV

*When our Lord* went up on high, He left His representative behind Him. This was Holy Church, His mystical Body and Bride, a Divine Institution, and the shrine and organ of the Paraclete, who speaks through

her till the end comes. She…is "His very self below,"
in so far as men on earth are equal to the discharge
and fulfilment of high offices, which primarily and
supremely are His.

*VIA MEDIA I*

*Commonly* the Church has nothing more to do than
to go on in her own proper duties, in confidence and
peace; to stand still and to see the salvation of God.

*ADDRESSES TO CARDINAL NEWMAN WITH HIS REPLIES*

*When the Church* does not speak, others will speak
instead.

*LOSS AND GAIN*

*A people's religion* is ever a corrupt religion, in
spite of the provisions of Holy Church. If she is to be
Catholic, you must admit within her net fish of every
kind, guests good and bad, vessels of gold, vessels of
earth.

*CERTAIN DIFFICULTIES FELT BY ANGLICANS IN
CATHOLIC TEACHING CONSIDERED II*

*As neither the* local rulers nor the pastors of the Church are impeccable in act nor infallible in judgment, I am not obliged to maintain that all ecclesiastical measures and permissions have ever been praiseworthy.

VIA MEDIA I (FROM THE 1877 PREFACE)

*A Prophet* is one who comes from God, who speaks with authority, who is ever one and the same, who is precise and decisive in his statements, who is equal to successive difficulties, and can smite and overthrow error. Such has the Catholic Church shown herself in her history.

DISCOURSES TO MIXED CONGREGATIONS

*Among all* the instances of unity, of harmony, and of law, which the Creator has given us…the most perfect is that which exists in His Church. In the music of her doctrines, in the wisdom of her precepts, in the majesty of her Hierarchy, in the beauty of her Ritual, in the luster of her Saints, in the consistent march of her policy…—in all of these we recognize the Hand of the God.

SERMONS PREACHED ON VARIOUS OCCASIONS

*The Church of Christ*…is not an institution of man, not a mere political establishment, not a creature of the state…made and unmade at its will, but it is a Divine society, a great work of God.

PAROCHIAL AND PLAIN SERMONS VII

*We did not make* the Church, we may not unmake it.

PAROCHIAL AND PLAIN SERMONS III

*A Catholic priest* has always a work to do, and a harvest to reap…Had he not confidence in the darkest day, and the most hostile district, he would be relinquishing a principal note of the Church. She is Catholic, because she brings a universal remedy for a universal disease. The disease is sin; all men have sinned; all men need a recovery in Christ.

DISCOURSES TO MIXED CONGREGATIONS

## 8.

# GOD:
## FATHER,
## SON, AND
## HOLY SPIRIT

*This world* is always changing, but God alone is unchanging: From the beginning, he is Father, Son, and Holy Spirit. The God of the Old Testament is the God of the New: he who revealed himself to the Jews is he who has revealed himself in Christ. The life of Christ on earth, he who is the Word of God, shows us what God is like: a God of compassion, but also a judge, who speaks of good and evil. God's love is shown in the humility of the Incarnation: he has become weak for our sakes, he has taken our infirmity, our temptations upon himself. And as Christ suffered death before returning to the Father in glory, so our lives are marked by the pain of the cross. But God works through this, through "means and ends, by steps, by victories hardly gained," so that he may bring us through the trials of this world into the peace and joy of his kingdom.

– L B

*I am a Catholic* by virtue of my believing in God; and if I am asked why I believe in a God, I answer that it is because I believe in myself, for I feel it impossible to believe in my own existence...without believing also in the existence of Him, who lives as a Personal, All-seeing, All-judging Being in my conscience.

APOLOGIA PRO VITA SUA

*Christ came*...to gather together in one all the elements of good dispersed throughout the world, to make them His own, to illuminate them with Himself, to reform and refashion them into Himself...He came to construct a new kingdom on the earth: that what had as yet lain in sin, might become what it was at the first...He took on Him our nature, that in God that nature might revive and be restored; that...after being perfect on the Cross, might impart that which itself was, as an incorruptible seed, for the life of all who receive it in faith.

LECTURES ON JUSTIFICATION

*When we confess God* as Omnipotent only, we have gained but a half-knowledge of Him: His is an Omnipotence which can at the same time swathe Itself in infirmity and can become the captive of Its own creatures. He has…the incomprehensible power of even making Himself weak. We must know Him by His names, Emmanuel and Jesus, to know Him perfectly.

SERMONS PREACHED ON VARIOUS OCCASIONS

*The heavenly gift* of the Spirit fixes the eyes of our mind upon the Divine Author of our salvation. By nature we are blind and carnal; but the Holy Ghost by whom we are new-born, reveals to us the God of mercies, and bids us adore Him as our Father with a true heart.

PAROCHIAL AND PLAIN SERMONS II

*Eternal Paraclete,* co-equal with the Father and Son…you are that living love, wherewith the Father and the Son love each other. And You are the Author of supernatural love in our hearts—As a fire You came down from heaven on the day of Pentecost; and as a fire You burn away the dross of sin and vanity in the heart...We are by nature blind and hard-hearted in all spiritual matters; how are we to reach heaven? It is by the flame of Your grace, O Almighty Paraclete.

*MEDITATIONS AND DEVOTIONS*

*Whereas God* is one, and His will one, and His purpose one, and His work one; whereas all He is and does is absolutely perfect and complete, independent of time and place, yet...in His actual dealings with this world...He seems to work by a process, by means and ends, by steps, by victories hardly gained, and failures repaired, and sacrifices ventured.

*PAROCHIAL AND PLAIN SERMONS II*

*The Creator* of this world is none other than the Father of our Lord Jesus Christ; there are not two Gods, one of matter, one of spirit; one of the Law, and one of the Gospel. There is one God, and He is Lord of all we are, and all we have; and, therefore, all we do must be stamped with His seal and signature.

*PAROCHIAL AND PLAIN SERMONS VI*

*He it was* who created the worlds; He it was who…
showed Himself to be a living and observant God,
whether men thought of Him or not. Yet this great
God condescended to come down on earth from His
heavenly throne, and to be born into His own world;
showing Himself as the Son of God in a new and
second sense, in a created nature, as well as in His
eternal substance.

PAROCHIAL AND PLAIN SERMONS V

*The fortunes* of the world change; what was high,
lies low; what was low rises high. Riches take wings
and flee away; bereavements happen. Friends become
enemies, and enemies friends. Our wishes, aims, and
plans change. There is nothing stable but You, O my
God! And You are the center and life of all…who
trust You as their Father [and]…are content to put
themselves into Your hands.

MEDITATIONS AND DEVOTIONS

*God beholds you* individually…He "calls you by name." He sees you, and understands you, as He made you. He knows what is in you, all your own peculiar feelings and thoughts, your dispositions and likings, your strength and your weakness. He views you in your day of rejoicing, and your day of sorrow. He sympathizes in your hopes and your temptations. He interests Himself in all your anxieties and remembrances, all the risings and fallings of your spirit.

PAROCHIAL AND PLAIN SERMONS III


*You alone, O God,* are what You ever have been. Man changes. You are unchangeable; even as man You were ever unchangeable, for Jesus is yesterday and today Himself, and for ever. Your word endures in heaven and earth. Your decrees are fixed…Your Nature, Your Attributes, are ever the same. There ever was Father, ever Son, ever Holy Ghost.

MEDITATIONS AND DEVOTIONS

9.

# THE MASS
# AND THE
# SACRAMENTS

*Let us* not underestimate the sacraments:
Through them, God himself acts directly in
this world, entering into our lives to bring
us his salvation. Baptism brings us into his
kingdom of light and frees us from slavery
to sin. The Mass brings us to the foot of his
Cross, sharing with Mary the wonderful graces
of his passion and death. The sacrament of
reconciliation, or confession, floods our souls
with the forgiveness of the risen Christ. In
all the sacraments, the heart of Christ beats
for us, beats with love for his children. So we
must approach the sacraments with reverence:
when we enter Church, we must be quiet and
prayerful; what happens in a Catholic Church
is greater and more mysterious than anything
else in this world.

–LB

*I could attend Masses* for ever and not be tired. It is not a mere form of words—it is…the greatest action that can be on earth. It is, not the invocation merely, but…the evocation of the Eternal. He becomes present on the altar in flesh and blood, before whom angels bow and devils tremble. This is that awful event which is the scope…of every part of the solemnity. Words are necessary, but as a means, not as ends; they are not mere addresses to the throne of grace, they are instruments of what is far higher, of consecration, of sacrifice.

LOSS AND GAIN


*If any one desires* illumination to know God's will as well as strength to do it, let him come to Mass daily. At least let him present himself daily before the Blessed Sacrament, and…offer his heart to His Incarnate Savior, presenting it as an offering to be influenced, changed and sanctified under the eye and by the grace of the Eternal Son.

FAITH AND PREJUDICE

*Holy Mother*, stand by me now at Mass time, when Christ comes to me, as you did minister to Your infant Lord—as you did hang upon His words when He grew up, as you were found under His cross. Stand by me, Holy Mother, so that I may gain somewhat of your purity, your innocence, your faith, and He may be the one object of my love and my adoration, as He was of yours.

*MEDITATIONS AND DEVOTIONS*

*He took bread,* and blessed, and made it His Body; He took wine and gave thanks, and made it His Blood; and He gave His priests the power to do what He had done. Henceforth, He is in the hands of sinners once more. Frail, ignorant, sinful man, by the sacerdotal power given to him, compels the presence of the Highest; he lays Him up in a small tabernacle; he dispenses Him to a sinful people.

*MEDITATIONS AND DEVOTIONS*

*Our Lord* not only offered Himself as a Sacrifice on the cross, but He makes Himself a perpetual, a daily Sacrifice…In the Holy Mass that one Sacrifice on the cross once offered is renewed, continued, applied to our benefit. He seems to say, "My cross was raised up 1800 years ago, and only for a few hours—and very few of my servants were present there—but I intend to bring millions into my Church. For their sakes, then, I will perpetuate My Sacrifice, so that each of them may be as though they had been present on Calvary.

MEDITATIONS AND DEVOTIONS

*How many* are the souls, in distress, anxiety or loneliness, whose one need is to find a being to whom they can pour out their feelings unheard by the world? Tell them out they must; they cannot tell them out to those whom they see every hour. They… wish to tell them to one who is strong enough to bear them, yet not too strong to despise them; they wish to tell them to one who can at once advise and can sympathize with them; they wish to relieve themselves of a load, to gain a solace…If there is a heavenly idea in the Catholic Church, surely, next after the Blessed Sacrament, Confession is such.

LECTURES ON THE PRESENT POSITION OF CATHOLICS IN ENGLAND

*Most loving Heart* of Jesus, You are concealed in the Holy Eucharist, and You are beating for us still.

MEDITATIONS AND DEVOTIONS

*This wonderful change* from darkness to light, through the entrance of the Spirit into the soul, is called…the New Birth; a blessing which, before Christ's coming, not even Prophets and the righteous possessed, but which is now conveyed to all freely through the Sacrament of Baptism.

PAROCHIAL AND PLAIN SERMONS II

*All we do* in Church is done on a principle of *reverence*; it is done with the thought that we are in God's presence.

PAROCHIAL AND PLAIN SERMONS VIII

*At times* we seem to catch a glimpse of a Form which we shall hereafter see face to face. We approach…We know not where we are, but we have been bathing in water, and a voice tells us that it is blood. Or we have a mark signed upon our foreheads, and it spoke of Calvary. Or we recollect a hand laid upon our heads, and surely it had the print of nails in it, and resembled His who with a touch gave sight to the blind...Or we have been eating and drinking; and it was not a dream surely, that One fed us from His wounded side, and renewed our nature by the heavenly meat He gave. Thus in many ways He, who is Judge to us, prepares us to be judged,—He, who is to glorify us, prepares us to be glorified.

PAROCHIAL AND PLAIN SERMONS V

*All Christians* are kings in God's sight; they are kings in His unseen kingdom, in His spiritual world, in the Communion of Saints. They seem like others, but they have crowns on their heads, and glorious robes around them, and Angels to wait on them, though our bodily eyes see it not. Such are all Christians, high and low; all Christians who remain in that state in which Holy Baptism placed them. Baptism placed you in this blessed state. God did not wait till you should do some good thing before He blessed you. No! He knew you could do no good thing of yourselves. So He came to you first; He loved you before you loved Him.

PAROCHIAL AND PLAIN SERMONS VIII

*You know*, O my God, who made us, that nothing can satisfy us but Yourself, and therefore You have caused Your own self to be meat and drink to us...You most Glorious, and Beautiful, and Strong, and Sweet, You know well that nothing else would support our immortal natures, our frail hearts, but Yourself; and so You did take a human flesh and blood, that they, as being the flesh and blood of God, might be our life.

MEDITATIONS AND DEVOTIONS

*Why do you believe* that our Lord rose from the dead? Why, that He redeemed us all with His precious blood? Why, that He washes away our sins in Baptism? Why do you believe in the power and grace which attends the other sacraments? Why do you believe in the resurrection of our bodies? You believe it because nothing is too hard for God—because however wonderful a thing may be, He can do it.

FAITH AND PREJUDICE

*Such are the arms* which faith uses, small in appearance…what seems a mere word, or a mere symbol, or mere bread and wine; but God has chosen the weak things of the world to confound the mighty, and foolish things of the world to confound the wise; and as all things spring from small beginnings, from seeds and elements invisible or insignificant, so when God would renew the race of man, and reverse the course of human life and earthly affairs, He chose cheap things for the rudiments of His work.

PAROCHIAL AND PLAIN SERMONS IV

*Not gold and silver,* jewels and fine linen, and skill of man to use them, make the House of God, but worshippers, the souls and bodies of those whom He has redeemed.

PAROCHIAL AND PLAIN SERMONS VI

10.

# OUR LADY,
# THE SAINTS,
# AND HEAVEN

*God's creation*, our universe, is truly beautiful. But heaven, the goal of the Christian which is already revealed to us in the Church, is more beautiful: There we will know the beauty of God, the beauty of the angels, the beatific vision. We are already citizens of heaven, but we are not yet ready. We must first become holy. The path has already been marked for us in the example of the saints and, supremely, in the example of the Blessed Virgin Mary. We must copy her faithfulness, her openness to prayer, her modesty, her purity. Faith points the way: We must not fear difficulty, we must put aside doubts about what God has promised, we must not fall away. Let us be true children of a loving Father so that we may meet him and love him forever.

–LB

*My Lord and Savior*, support me in that hour in the strong arms of Your Sacraments…Let the absolving words be said over me, and the holy oil sign and seal me, and Your own Body be my food, and Your Blood my sprinkling; and let my Mother, Mary, breathe on me, and my Angel whisper peace to me, and my glorious Saints…smile upon me; that in them all, and through them all, I may receive the gift of perseverance, and die, as I desire to live, in Your faith, in Your Church,…and in Your love. Amen.

MEDITATIONS AND DEVOTIONS

*To practice* a heavenly life on earth…is like trying to execute some high and refined harmony on an insignificant instrument. In attempting it, that instrument would be taxed beyond its powers, and would be sacrificed to great ideas beyond itself. And so, in a certain sense, this life, and our present nature, is sacrificed for heaven and the new creature; that while our outward man perishes, our inward man may be renewed day by day.

SERMONS BEARING ON THE SUBJECTS OF THE DAY

*I fully grant* that devotion towards the blessed Virgin has increased among Catholics with the progress of centuries; I do not allow that the doctrine concerning her has undergone a growth, for I believe that it has been in substance one and the same from the beginning.

CERTAIN DIFFICULTIES FELT BY ANGLICANS IN CATHOLIC TEACHING CONSIDERED II

*Who can live* any time in the world, pleasant as it may seem on first entering it, without discovering that it is a weariness, and that if this life is worth any thing, it is because it is the passage to another? It needs no great religion to feel this; it is a self-evident truth.

PAROCHIAL AND PLAIN SERMONS VII

*The earth* that we see does not satisfy us; it is but a beginning; it is but a promise of something beyond it...We know much more lies hid in it than we see. A world of Saints and Angels, a glorious world, the palace of God, the mountain of the Lord of Hosts, the heavenly Jerusalem, the throne of God and Christ, all these wonders, everlasting, mysterious, and incomprehensible, lie hid in what we see. What we see is the outward shell of an eternal kingdom; and on that kingdom we fix the eyes of our faith.

PAROCHIAL AND PLAIN SERMONS IV

*Such are the feelings* with which men often look back on their childhood, when any accident brings …them back in memory to the first years of their discipleship; and they then see, what they could not know at the time, that God's presence went up with them and gave them rest…They are full of tender, affectionate thoughts towards those first years, but they do not know why. They think it is those very years which they yearn after, whereas it is the presence of God which, as they now see, was then over them, which attracts them. They think that they regret the past, when they are but longing after the future. It is not that they would be children again, but that they would be Angels and would see God; they would be immortal beings…robed in white, and with palms in their hands, before His throne.

PAROCHIAL AND PLAIN SERMONS IV

*What a day* will that be when I am thoroughly cleansed from all impurity and sin, and am fit to draw near to my Incarnate God in His palace of light above!

MEDITATIONS AND DEVOTIONS

*Mary*…is pre-eminently faithful to her Lord and Son. Let no one for an instant suppose that she is not supremely zealous for His honor, or…that to exalt her is to be unfaithful to Him. Her true servants are still more truly His. Well as she rewards her friends, she would deem him no friend, but a traitor, who preferred her to Him.

MEDITATIONS AND DEVOTIONS

*There have been ages* of the world, in which men have thought too much of Angels, and paid them excessive honor; honored them so perversely as to forget the supreme worship due to Almighty God. This is the sin of a dark age. But the sin of an educated age, such as our own, is just the reverse: to account slightly of them, or not at all; to ascribe all we see around us, not to their agency, but to certain assumed laws of nature.

PAROCHIAL AND PLAIN SERMONS II

*There is no part* of the history of Jesus but Mary has her part in it.

MEDITATIONS AND DEVOTIONS

*My dear and holy* Patron, Philip [Neri], I put myself into your hands, and for the love of Jesus, for that love's sake which chose you and made you a saint, I implore you to pray for me, that, as He has brought you to heaven, so in due time He may take me to heaven too.

MEDITATIONS AND DEVOTIONS

*[A saint] differs* from an ordinary religious man, I say in this,—that he sets before him as the one object of life, to please and obey God; that he ever aims to submit his will to God's will; that he earnestly follows after holiness; and that he is habitually striving to have a closer resemblance to Christ in all things. He exercises himself, not only in social duties, but in Christian graces; he is not only kind, but meek; not only generous, but humble; not only persevering, but patient; not only upright, but forgiving; not only bountiful, but self-denying; not only contented, but meditative and devotional.

PAROCHIAL AND PLAIN SERMONS IV

*When God would prepare* a human mother for His Son…He began by giving her an immaculate conception. He began, not by giving her the gift of love, or truthfulness, or gentleness, or devotion, though according to the occasion she had them all. But He began His great work before she was born; before she could think, speak, or act, by making her *holy*, and thereby, while on earth, a citizen of heaven.

MEDITATIONS AND DEVOTIONS

*After the fever* of life; after wearinesses and sicknesses; fightings and despondings; languor and fretfulness; struggling and failing, struggling and succeeding; after all the changes and chances of this troubled unhealthy state, at length comes death, at length the White Throne of God, at length the Beatific Vision.

PAROCHIAL AND PLAIN SERMONS VI

*If the Mother* of Emmanuel ought to be the first of creatures in sanctity; if it became her to be free from all sin from the very first; and if such was her beginning, such was her end, her conception immaculate and her death an assumption; but what is befitting in the children of such a Mother, but an imitation of her devotion, her meekness, her simplicity, her modesty, and her sweetness? Her glories are not only for the sake of her Son, they are for our sakes also. Let us copy her faith, who received God's message by the angel without a doubt; her patience, who endured Saint Joseph's surprise without a word; her obedience, who went up to Bethlehem in the winter and bore our Lord in a stable; her meditative spirit, who pondered in her heart what she saw and heard about Him; her fortitude whose heart the sword went through; her self-surrender, who gave Him up during His ministry and consented to his death.

DISCOURSES TO MIXED CONGREGATIONS

*The Blessed Virgin* is called All-Powerful because she has, more than anyone else, more than all Angels and Saints, this great gift of prayer. No one has access to the Almighty as His Mother has; none has merit such as hers. Her Son will deny her nothing that she asks; and herein lies her power. While she defends the Church, neither height nor depth, neither men nor evil spirits, neither great monarchs, nor craft of man, nor popular violence, can avail to harm us; for human life is short, but Mary reigns above, a Queen for ever.

MEDITATIONS AND DEVOTION

## II.

# DOCTRINE
## AND ITS
## DEVELOPMENT

*What are* doctrines? They are the truths of our faith expressed in human language. They are developed over centuries by the Popes and Ecumenical Councils, the result of meditation on the Scriptures, of prayer, and of the guidance of the Holy Spirit. They help us better know and live our faith. So, as time passes, the Church grows in her understanding of the faith. Newman is a supreme witness to the *development* of doctrine, the idea that some truths lay hidden in the depths of the Church, to come into the light in later centuries. For instance, the Immaculate Conception of Our Lady wasn't defined as a doctrine until 1854. But that doesn't mean it's a new idea: It was true from the beginning. So development of doctrine isn't when the Church changes its mind. On the contrary, she speaks her mind with ever greater force.

–LB

*The world is full* of doubtings and uncertainty, and of inconsistent doctrine—a clear consistent idea of revealed truth, on the contrary, cannot be found outside of the Catholic Church.

*FAITH AND PREJUDICE*

*It may seem* a contradiction in terms to call Revelation a Mystery…How is this? The answer is simple. No revelation can be complete and systematic, from the weakness of the human intellect; so far as it is not such, it is mysterious. When nothing is revealed, nothing is known, and there is nothing to contemplate; but when something is revealed, and only something, for all cannot be revealed, there are forthwith difficulties and perplexities.

*ESSAYS CRITICAL AND HISTORICAL I*

*When Providence* would make a Revelation, He does not begin anew, but uses the existing system; He does not visibly send an Angel, but He commissions one of our own....When He would consecrate us, He takes the elements of this world as the means of real but unseen spiritual influences. When He would set up a divine polity, He takes a polity which already is...Nor does He interfere with its natural growth or dependence on things visible. He does not shut it up in a desert, and there supply it with institutions unlike those which might naturally come to it from the contact...of the external world. He does but modify, quicken, or direct the powers of nature or the laws of society...Thus the great characteristic of Revelation is addition, substitution.

*Essays Critical and Historical II*

*If Christianity* be an universal religion, suited... to all times and places, it cannot but vary in its relations and dealings towards the world around it, that is, it will develop. Principles require a very various application according as persons and circumstances vary, and must be thrown into new shapes according to the form of society which they are to influence...

The refutation and remedy of errors cannot precede their rise; and thus the fact of false developments or corruptions involves the correspondent manifestation of true ones.

*Christianity is faith,* faith implies a doctrine; a doctrine propositions; propositions yes or no, yes or no differences. Differences, then, are the natural attendants on Christianity, and you cannot have Christianity, and not have differences.

*Mary is our pattern* of Faith, both in the reception and in the study of Divine Truth. She does not think it enough to accept, she dwells upon it; not enough to possess, she uses it; not enough to assent, she develops it; not enough to submit the Reason, she reasons upon it; not indeed reasoning first, and believing afterwards...yet first believing without reasoning, next from love and reverence, reasoning after believing.

*The notion* of doctrinal knowledge absolutely novel, and of simple addition from without, is intolerable to Catholic ears, and never was entertained by any one who was even approaching to an understanding of our creed. Revelation is all in all in doctrine; the Apostles its sole depository...and ecclesiastical authority its sole sanction. The Divine Voice has spoken once for all.

*IDEA OF A UNIVERSITY*

*Revelation* consists in the manifestation of the Invisible Divine Power, or in the substitution of the voice of a Lawgiver for the voice of conscience. The supremacy of conscience is the essence of natural religion; the supremacy of Apostle, or Pope, or Church, or Bishop, is the essence of revealed [religion].

*ESSAY ON THE DEVELOPMENT OF DOCTRINE*

*The Catholic Creed,* as coming from God, is so harmonious, so consistent with itself, holds together so perfectly, so corresponds part to part, that an acute mind, knowing one portion of it, would often infer another portion, merely as a matter of just reasoning.

*DISCOURSES TO MIXED CONGREGATIONS*

*True* is it the Gospels will do very much by way of realizing for us the incarnation of the Son of God, if studied in faith and love. But the Creeds are an additional help. The declarations made in them… supported and illuminated by Scripture, draw down from heaven, the image of Him who is on God's right hand…and rouse in us those mingled feelings of fear and confidence, affection and devotion towards Him, which are implied in the belief of a personal advent of God in our nature, and which were originally derived to the Church from the very sight of Him.

PAROCHIAL AND PLAIN SERMONS II

*The body* of the faithful is one of the witnesses to the fact of the tradition of revealed doctrine.

ON CONSULTING THE FAITHFUL IN
MATTERS OF DOCTRINE

*In most cases* when a [doctrinal] definition is contemplated, the laity will have a testimony to give; but if ever there be an instance when they ought to be consulted, it is in the case of doctrines which bear directly upon devotional sentiments. Such is the Immaculate Conception.

ON CONSULTING THE FAITHFUL IN
MATTERS OF DOCTRINE

*Gradually* and in the course of ages, Catholic inquiry has taken certain definite shapes, and has thrown itself into the form of a science, with a method and a phraseology of its own, under the intellectual handling of great minds, such as Saint Athanasius, Saint Augustine, and Saint Thomas; and I feel no temptation at all to break in pieces the great legacy of thought thus committed to us.

*ESSAY ON THE DEVELOPMENT OF DOCTRINE*

*What do we gain* from words, however correct and abundant, if they end with themselves, instead of lighting up the image of the Incarnate Son in our hearts?

*PAROCHIAL AND PLAIN SERMONS III*

*If the very claim* to infallible arbitration in religious disputes is of so weighty importance...in all ages of the world, much more is it welcome at a time like the present, when the human intellect is so busy, and thought so fertile, and opinion so manifold. The absolute need of a spiritual supremacy is at present the strongest of arguments in favor of the fact of its supply.

*ESSAY ON THE DEVELOPMENT OF DOCTRINE*

*No one doctrine* can be named which starts complete at first, and gains nothing afterwards from the investigations of faith and the attacks of heresy.

ESSAY ON THE DEVELOPMENT OF DOCTRINE

*In a higher world* it is otherwise, but here below to live is to change, and to be perfect is to have changed often.

ESSAY ON THE DEVELOPMENT OF DOCTRINE

12.

# Catholic
# Education,
# Politics,
# and History

*What do* history and society have to do with Christianity? Everything. Because the Church serves Christ in this world, she lives amid the fortunes of nations and peoples, she bears the mark of history. The Church shares the challenges of the whole human family. But, Newman emphasizes, the Church has her own mission: to worship and serve God in a world where he often seems to be absent. She can't be reduced to a social agency or, what is more terrible, an instrument of the state. This is one reason Christian education is essential: It teaches us to understand our faith and how it relates to this world, so that we can be Catholics who not only believe what the Church teaches, but also show how our religion applies to the problems of our age.

–LB

*It is one* great advantage of an age in which unbelief speaks out, that Faith can speak out too; that, if falsehood assails Truth, Truth can assail falsehood. In such an age it is possible to found a University more emphatically Catholic than could be set up in the middle age, because Truth can entrench itself carefully, and define its own profession severely, and display its colors unequivocally, by occasion of that very unbelief which so shamelessly vaunts itself.

*IDEA OF A UNIVERSITY*

*It will not* satisfy me [in a university]…to have two independent systems, intellectual and religious, going at once side by side, by a sort of division of labor, and only accidentally brought together. It will not satisfy me, if religion is here, and science there, and young men converse with science all day, and lodge with religion in the evening. It is not touching the evil to which these remarks have been directed if young men eat and drink and sleep in one place, and think in another: I want the same roof to contain both the intellectual and moral discipline. Devotion is not a sort of finish given to the sciences; nor is science a sort of feather in the cap…and set-off to devotion. I want the intellectual layman to be religious, and the devout ecclesiastic to be intellectual.

SERMONS PREACHED ON VARIOUS OCCASIONS

*No conclusion* is trustworthy which has not been tried by enemy as well as friend; no traditions have a claim upon us which shrink from criticism, and dare not look a rival in the face.

LECTURES ON THE PRESENT POSITION OF
CATHOLICS IN ENGLAND

*He who can realize* the law of moral conflicts, and the incoherence of falsehood, and the issue of perplexities, and the end of all things, and the Presence of the Judge, becomes, from the very necessity of the case,  philosophical, long-suffering, and magnanimous.

LECTURES ON THE PRESENT POSITION OF
CATHOLICS IN ENGLAND

*Here are two injuries* which Revelation is likely to sustain at the hands of the Masters of human reason unless the Church, as in duty bound, protects the sacred treasure…The first is a simple ignoring of Theological Truth altogether, under the pretense of not recognizing differences of religious opinion… The second, which is of a more subtle character, is a recognition indeed of Catholicism, but (as if in pretended mercy to it) an adulteration of its spirit.

IDEA OF A UNIVERSITY

*In order* to teach well, more must be learned by the teacher than he has formally to impart to the pupil; that he must be above his work, and know, and know accurately and philosophically, what he does not actually profess.

HISTORICAL SKETCHES III

*Narrow minds have* no power of throwing themselves into the minds of others. They have stiffened in one position, as limbs of the body subjected to confinement…They have already parcelled out to their own satisfaction the whole world of knowledge; they have drawn their lines, and formed their classes, and given to each opinion, argument, principle, and party, its own locality.

OXFORD UNIVERSITY SERMONS

*To be dispassionate* and cautious, to be fair in discussion, to give to each phenomenon which nature successively presents its due weight, candidly to admit those which militate against our own theory, to be willing to be ignorant for a time, to submit to difficulties, and patiently and meekly proceed, waiting for farther light…is the very temper which Christianity sets forth as the perfection of our moral character.

OXFORD UNIVERSITY SERMONS

*Nothing is more common* than for men to think that because they are familiar with words, they understand the ideas they stand for. Educated persons…fall into the same error in a more subtle form, when they think they understand terms used in morals and religion, because such are common words, and have been used by them all their lives.

PAROCHIAL AND PLAIN SERMONS I

*To open the mind,* to correct it, to refine it, to enable it to know…and use its knowledge, to give it power over its own faculties…[is] an object as intelligible as the cultivation of virtue, while, at the same time, it is absolutely distinct from it.

IDEA OF A UNIVERSITY

*It does,* in matter of fact, act to the disadvantage of a Christian place of education,…in the judgment of men of the world, and is a reproach to its conductors, and even a scandal, if it sends out its pupils accomplished in all knowledge except Christian knowledge.

IDEA OF A UNIVERSITY

*Christianity* has raised the tone of morals, has restrained the passions, and enforced external decency and good conduct in the world at large; it has advanced certain persons in virtuous or religious habits;…it has given a firmness and consistency to religious profession in numbers, and perhaps has extended the range of really religious practice. Still on the whole the great multitude of men have to all appearance remained, in a spiritual point of view, no better than before.

PAROCHIAL AND PLAIN SERMONS IV

*The direct* and prime aim of the Church is the worship of the Unseen God; the sole object, as I may say, of the social and political world everywhere, is to make the most of this life.

LETTER TO JOHN MOZLEY, DEC. 3, 1875

*Human Society, indeed,* is an ordinance of God;... but from the first an enemy has been busy in its depravation. Hence it is, that while in its substance it is divine, in its circumstances, tendencies, and results it has much of evil. Never do men come together in considerable numbers, but the passion, self-will, pride, and unbelief, which may be more or less dormant in them one by one, bursts into a flame, and becomes a constituent of their union.

SERMONS PREACHED ON VARIOUS OCCASIONS

*I am not* so irrational as to despise Public Opinion... It has its place in the very constitution of society; it ever has existed...whether in the commonwealth of nations, or in the humble and secluded village. But wholesome as it is as a principle, it has, in common with all things human, great imperfections, and makes many mistakes.

HISTORICAL SKETCHES III

*The noblest efforts* of [man's] genius, the conquests he has made, the doctrines he has originated, the nations he has civilized, the states he has created...

they outlive him by many centuries, but they tend to an end, and that end is dissolution. Powers of the world, sovereignties, dynasties, sooner or later come to nought; they have their fatal hour.

SERMONS PREACHED ON VARIOUS OCCASIONS

*Faith has no leisure* to act as [does] the busy politician, to...demand rights, to flatter the many, or to court the powerful.

PAROCHIAL AND PLAIN SERMONS III

*Those men* are not necessarily the most useful men in their generation, not the most favored by God, who make the most noise in the world, and who seem to be principals in the great changes and events recorded in history.

PAROCHIAL AND PLAIN SERMONS II

*There must be* something wrong among us; when our defenders recommend the Church on the mere plea of its activity, its popularity, and its visible usefulness.

PAROCHIAL AND PLAIN SERMONS III

*No idea or principle* of political society includes in its operation all conceivable good, or excludes all evil; that is the best form of society which has most of the good, and least of the bad.

DISCUSSIONS AND ARGUMENTS

*Life in this world* is motion, and involves a continual process of change. Living things grow into their perfection, into their decline, into their death. No rule of art will suffice to stop the operation of this natural law, whether in the material world or in the human mind.

CERTAIN DIFFICULTIES FELT BY ANGLICANS IN CATHOLIC TEACHING CONSIDERED II

*Let all those* who acknowledge the voice of God speaking within them, and urging them heaven-ward, wait patiently for the End, exercising themselves, and diligently working, with a view to that day when the books shall be opened, and all the disorder of human affairs reviewed and set right.

OXFORD UNIVERSITY SERMONS

*Our first duty* is towards our Lord and His Church, and our second towards our earthly Sovereign.

PAROCHIAL AND PLAIN SERMONS VI

*It is very plain* that matters which agitate us most extremely now, will a year hence interest us not at all; that objects about which we have intense hope and fear now, will then be to us nothing more than things which happen at the other end of the earth. So will it be with all human hopes, fears, pleasures, pains, jealousies, disappointments, successes, when the last day is come.

PAROCHIAL AND PLAIN SERMONS V

# Sources

These works of John Henry Cardinal Newman were quoted in this book:

*Addresses to Cardinal Newman With His Replies.* London: Longmans, Green. 1905.

*Apologia Pro Vita Sua.* London: J. M. Dent. 1912.

*Certain Difficulties Felt by Anglicans in Catholic Teaching Considered.* London, New York: Longmans, Green. 1901. 2 vols.

*Discourses Addressed to Mixed Congregations.* London, New York: Longmans, Green. 1902.

*Discussions and Arguments on Various Subjects.* London, New York: Longmans, Green. 1918.

*An Essay in Aid of a Grammar of Assent.* London: Burns, Oates. 1870.

*Essays Critical and Historical.* London, New York: Longmans, Green. 1901. 2 vols.

*Faith and Prejudice and Other Unpublished Sermons of Cardinal Newman* edited by the Birmingham Oratory. New York: Sheed and Ward. nd.

*Fifteen Sermons Preached Before the University of Oxford Between A.D. 1826 and 1843.* London, New York: Longmans, Green. 1918.

*Historical Sketches.* London, New York: Longmans, Green. 1901-1903. 3 vols.

*The Idea of a University Defined and Illustrated.* London, New York: Longmans, Green. 1912.

*Lectures on the Doctrine of Justification*. London, New York: Longmans, Green. 1900.

*Lectures on the Present Position of Catholics in England*. London, New York: Longmans, Green. 1903.

*Loss and Gain: The Story of a Convert*. London, New York: Longmans, Green. 1903.

*Meditations and Devotions of the Late Cardinal Newman*. New York and London: Longmans, Green. 1893.

*On Consulting the Faithful in Matters of Doctrine*. New York: Sheed and Ward. 1962.

*On the Inspiration of Scripture*. Washington: Corpus Books. 1967. Holmes, J. Derek and Robert Murray, eds.

*Parochial and Plain Sermons*. London, New York: Longmans, Green. 1900. 8 vols.

*The Via Media of the Anglican Church*. London: Longmans, Green. 1901-1908. 2 vols.

*Sermons Bearing on the Subjects of the Day*. New York, London: Longmans, Green. 1918, 1843.

*Sermons Preached on Various Occasions*. London: Burns, Oates. 1874.